See th
Firefight

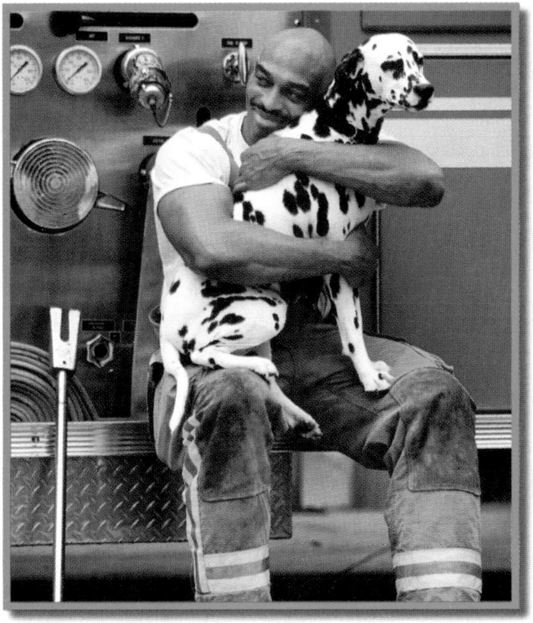

by Margie Sigman

HAMPTON-BROWN

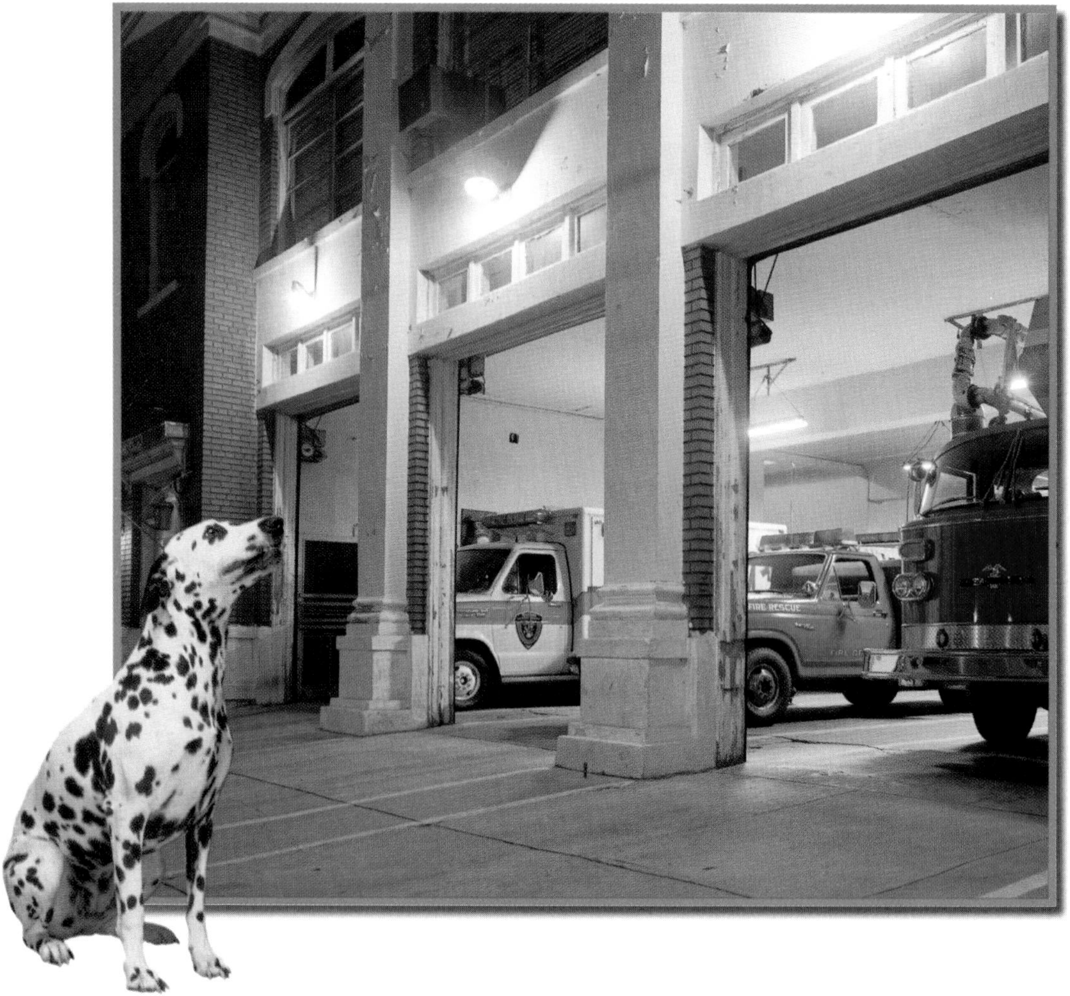

See the fire station.

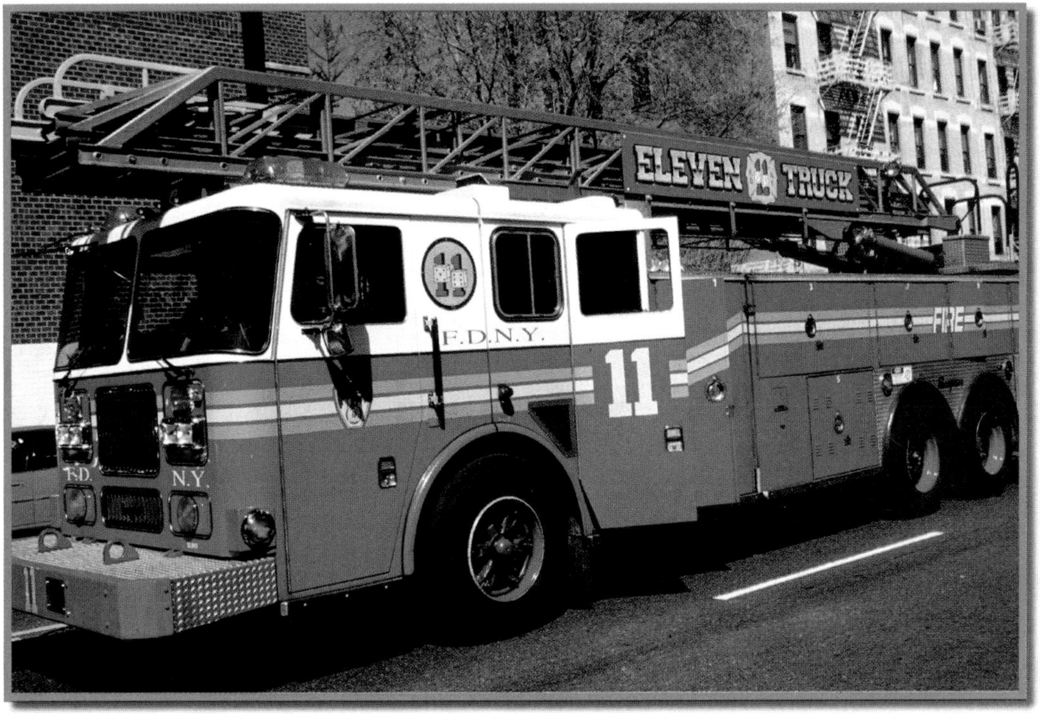

See the fire truck.

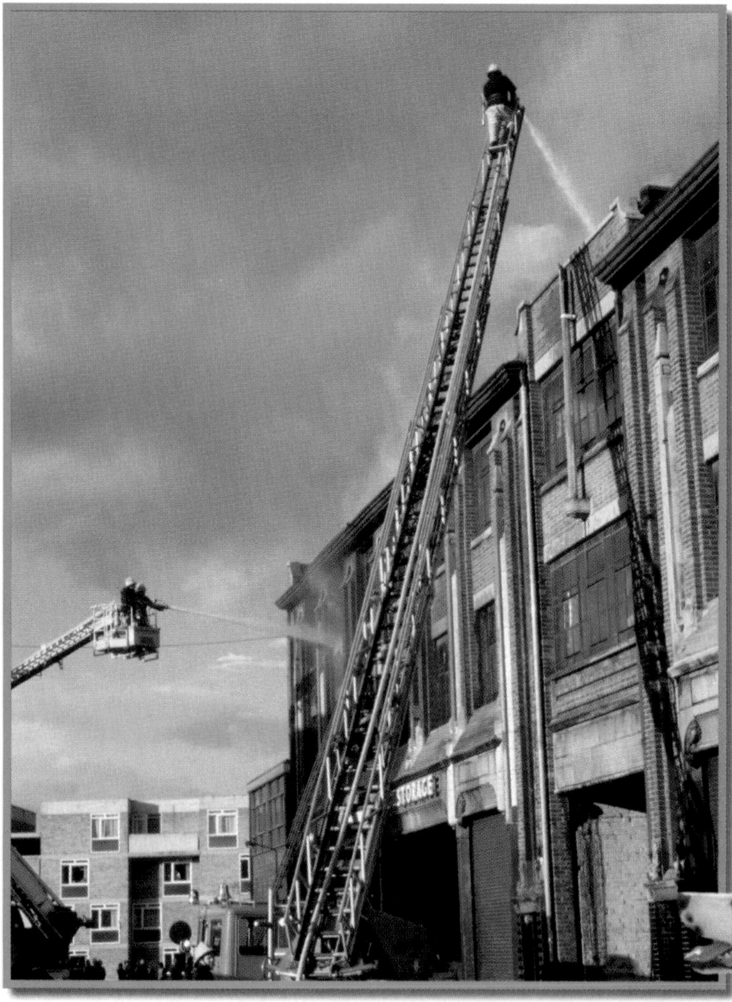

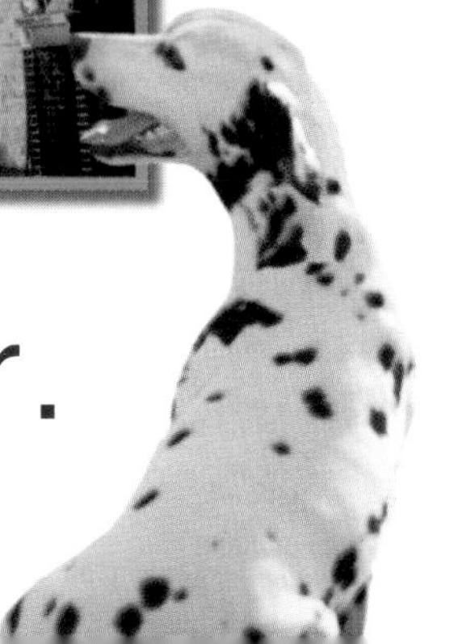

See the ladder.

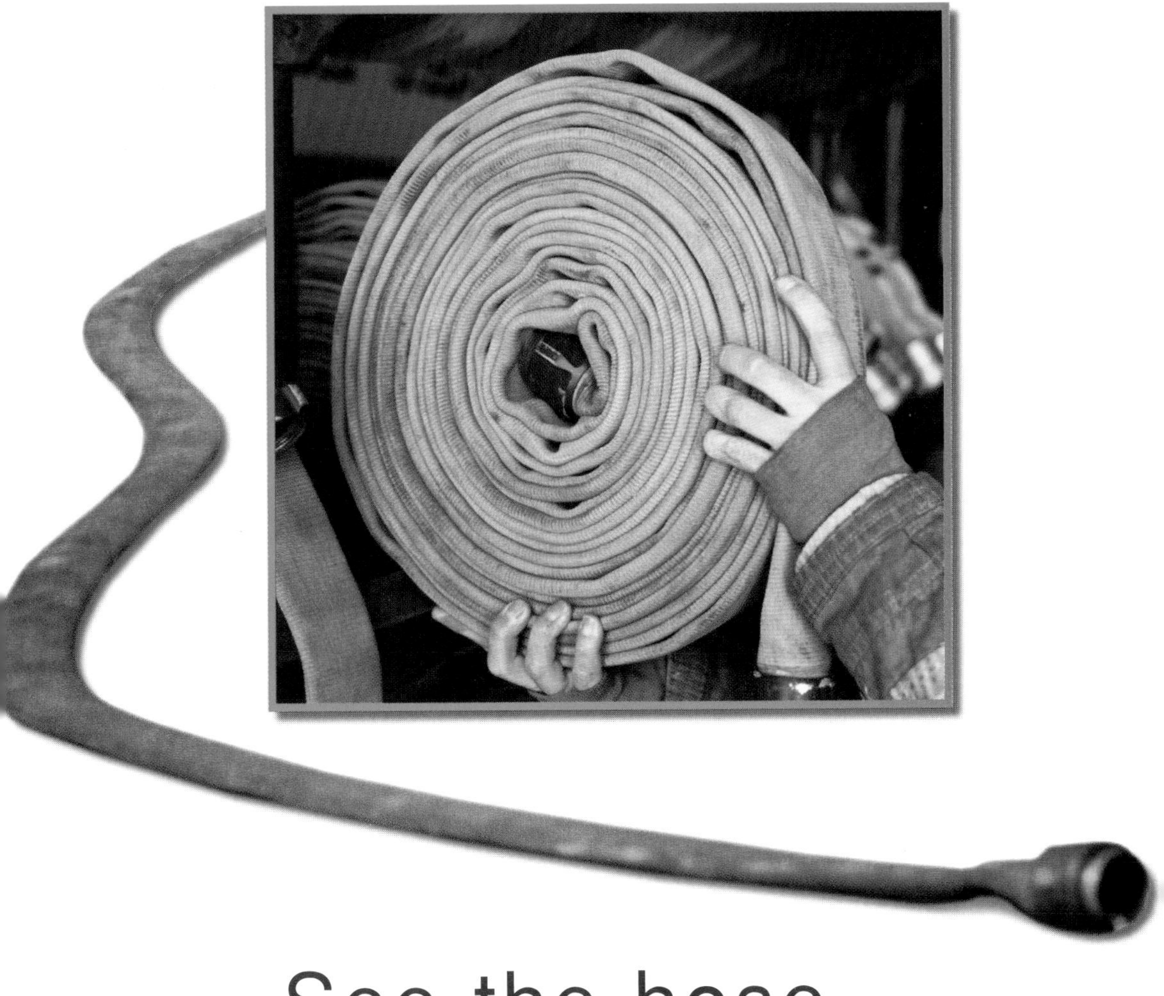

See the hose.

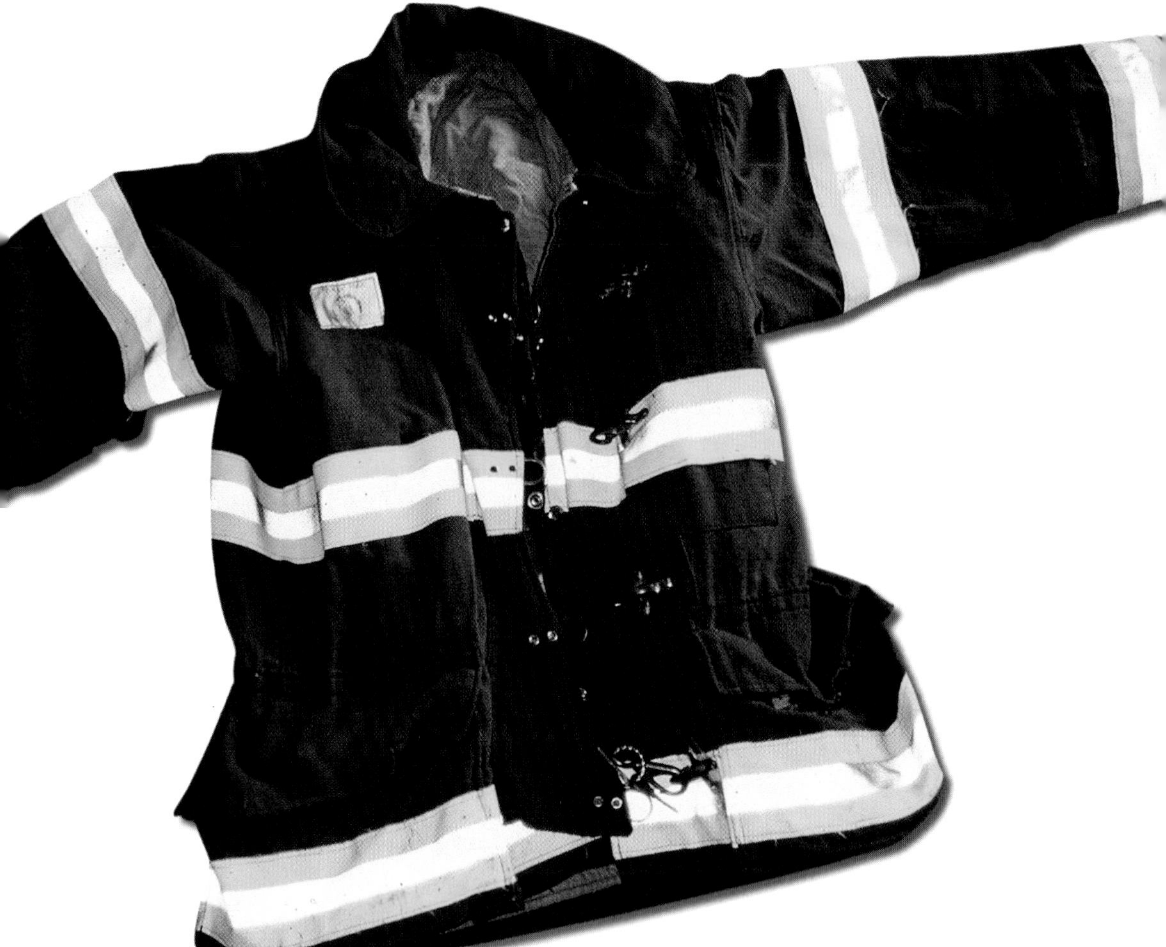

See the jacket.

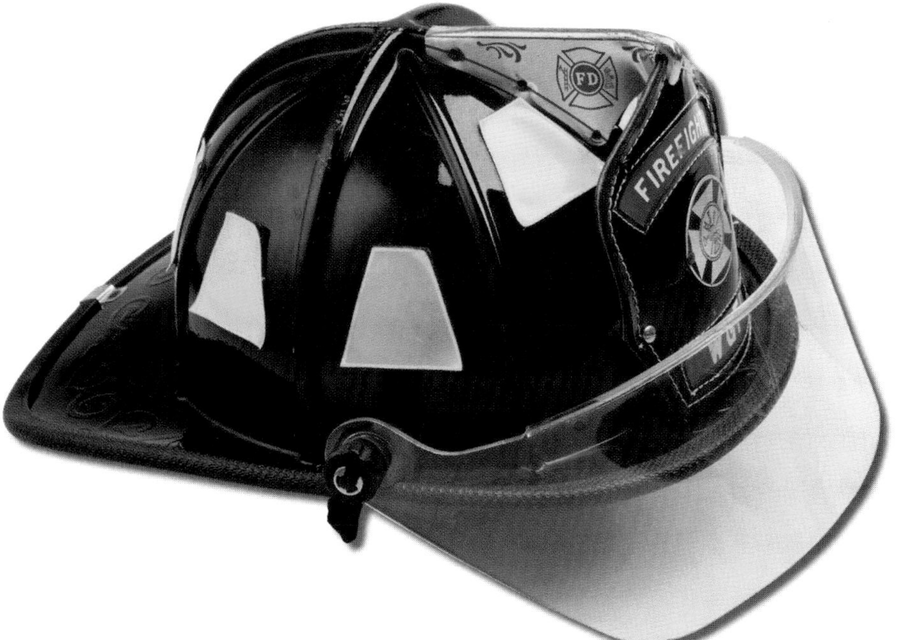

See the hat.

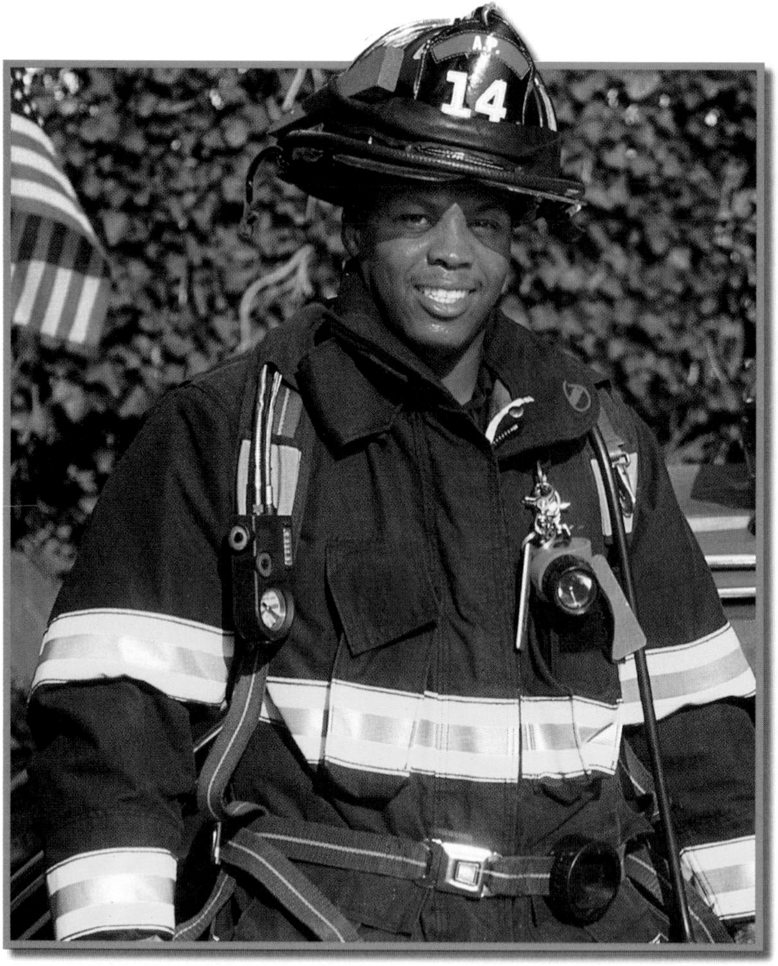

See the firefighter!